ART and
INVENTION

Inventions in the Visual Arts

From Cave Paintings to CAD

Cory MacPherson

Cavendish
Square

New York

Published in 2017 by Cavendish Square Publishing, LLC
243 5th Avenue, Suite 136, New York, NY 10016

Website: cavendishsq.com

This publication represents the opinions and views of the author based on his or her personal experience, knowledge, and research. The information in this book serves as a general guide only. The author and publisher have used their best efforts in preparing this book and disclaim liability rising directly or indirectly from the use and application of this book.

CPSIA Compliance Information: Batch #CW17CSQ

All websites were available and accurate when this book was sent to press.

Library of Congress Cataloging-in-Publication Data

Names: MacPherson, Cory, author.
Title: Inventions in the visual arts : from cave paintings to CAD / Cory MacPherson.
Description: New York : Cavendish Square Publishing, 2017. | Series: Art and invention | Includes bibliographical references and index.
Identifiers: LCCN 2016033398 (print) | LCCN 2016033885 (ebook) | ISBN 9781502623034 (library bound) | ISBN 9781502623041 (E-book)
Subjects: LCSH: Art and technology. | Artists' tools. | Artists' materials.
Classification: LCC N72.T4 M33 2017 (print) | LCC N72.T4 (ebook) | DDC 701/.05--dc23
LC record available at https://lccn.loc.gov/2016033398
Editorial Director: David McNamara
Editor: Caitlyn Miller
Copy Editor: Nathan Heidelberger
Associate Art Director: Amy Greenan
Designer: Joseph Macri
Production Assistant: Karol Szymczuk
Photo Research: J8 Media

Printed in the United States of America

CONTENTS

INTRODUCTION:
The Art of Seeing

The Greek philosopher Plato uses vision as a metaphor for knowledge in his famous cave allegory. His character (the historical figure Socrates) describes a group of prisoners in a dark cave, forced to look straight ahead: "From the beginning people like this have never managed, whether on their own or with the help by others, to see anything besides the shadows." Because they could not turn around, they could not see the actual objects, and therefore they thought the shadows of the objects were the objects themselves.

Our ability to see is directly related to our ability to know, and our eyes are our main tools to gain knowledge. But, like all tools, our eyes have limitations. So how do we learn about what we do not know? This question has led to many inventions in visual art, and in fact, visual art itself has extended our ability to understand what we see (and don't see).

Consider Galileo Galilei, a man who looked at the night sky in disbelief. He could not have imagined the solar system or that stars were balls of fire rather than twinkling lights, but he did imagine that the sky held more than he could see with his own eye. In 1633, he pointed a telescope toward the heavens and saw craters on the moon and the ribbons of light that make the Milky Way. What he saw changed what we know about Earth—that it revolves around the sun instead of the other way around, which was the common belief up until his time.

In 1889, another man looked at the night sky in disbelief. He too imagined the sky held more than could be seen with his eye. With a brush and canvas, he looked to the moon and ribbons of light that make the Milky Way, and painted the heavens. Unlike Galileo, Vincent van Gogh was searching for an intangible unseen, a divine power. He said, "It would be so simple and would account so much for the terrible things in life, which now amaze and wound us so, if life had yet another hemisphere, invisible it is true, but where one lands when one dies." Perhaps *The Starry Night* didn't change our view of the world in the way of Galileo, but the painting is similar in the way that it expands our perspective. In it, we see the enormity of the cosmos. And perhaps the two men were searching for the same thing after all. Galileo said, "Philosophy [Nature] is written in that great book which ever is before our eyes—I mean the universe—but we cannot understand it if we do not first learn the language and grasp the symbols in which it is written." Galileo was referring to the language of math, but ultimately he was reaching for a bigger understanding of the world, just as artists like Van Gogh do.

This impulse stretches back to the beginning of man. Ancient civilizations used paint on cave walls as a part of hunting or fertility rituals—visual art was more than just a **depiction** of their life, it was *part* of their life, a way to honor a higher power and ensure good fortune in their future. Likewise, ancient sculpture was used as a spiritual medium—statues of **deities** were used to communicate

Vincent van Gogh believed that painters taught the world how to see nature.

with the gods, and sculptures of the human body were used to express perfect beauty.

Artists from ancient Greece had the idea that math, specifically proportion, was the best way to design a sculpture that was a realistic portrayal of the human body. Today, architects and designers use this concept to create digital models so that they know how to build the most energy-efficient building or the fastest car without the expensive and time-consuming process of physical experimentation. Sketchbooks play a big part in modern civilization in a similar way because they also allow us to see ideas with our eyes instead of in our minds. When sketchbooks were invented, ideas became more like real things—images drawn on paper replaced the model images formed from clay. Sketchbooks perhaps even changed the way we think, and today creative types use the scientific method to refine and better understand their ideas. To writers, fashion designers, musicians, football coaches, and many more creative thinkers, experimentation is called revision or drafting instead of the scientific process, but both begin with observation and approach investigation using trial and error.

Of course, we understand now that photography, like drawing, is also representative. Our perception of reality again changed when the photograph was invented. Maybe this is partially because once the film camera was invented, we knew how the water looked at Niagara Falls, for example, without traveling there to see it in person. However, it is important to point out that the camera didn't replace the eye or the imagination as visual instruments because, as we already know, the camera was not necessarily more reliable or accurate. The camera changed the world because it showed us the limits of our eyesight and the inaccuracy of our imagination. In other words, in an age of photography, seeing is believing. With computer-aided design, the reverse is true: digital animation and 3D modeling programs make it possible to create the visions of our imagination.

The next six chapters will trace artists and scientists throughout history as they searched for ways to see the unseen, to know what was unknown—a darkness made light with the flash of a camera.

The outlined hands on the caves in South Sulawesi are nearly forty thousand years old.

CHAPTER 1
Cave Painting

While the rock axes and obsidian spearheads that date from tens of thousands of years ago may seem foreign to us, the art that these prehistoric people left speaks across time. These objects show us a spirit we can recognize today as essentially human, essentially ours. The first artists chose to depict mostly large animals—oxen, reindeer, horses, deer, rhinoceroses, pigs, and buffalo. They also sketched full human figures on cave walls and traced outlines of their hands. Art is the medium that tells the human story. In the fluid lines and dramatic shapes painted on cave walls, we can see a bit of the truth of prehistoric life shine through.

We do not know for certain the purpose of the ancient cave art. Were they painted by religious shamans as part of a trance? Or by hunters hoping to return with meat for their families? Or as a mark of power, a grand "I was here"? It's easy to see the many differences that separate us from prehistoric people, but just as the earliest painters depicted animals they observed, the animals in Pablo Picasso's *Guernica* (1937) are images taken from the artist's real life. Of the painting, he said:

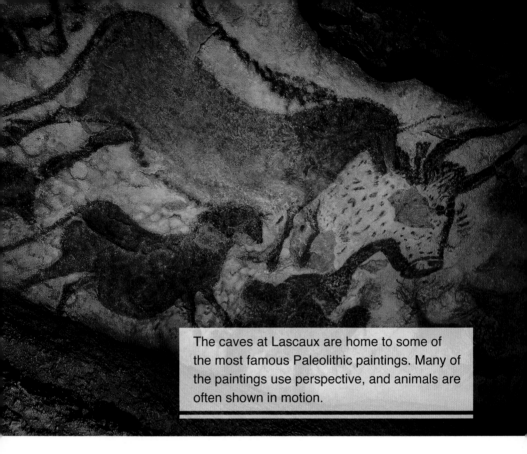

The caves at Lascaux are home to some of the most famous Paleolithic paintings. Many of the paintings use perspective, and animals are often shown in motion.

This bull is a bull and this horse is a horse … If you give a meaning to certain things in my paintings it may be very true, but it is not my idea to give this meaning. What ideas and conclusions you have got I obtained too, but instinctively, unconsciously. I make the painting for the painting. I paint the objects for what they are.

Can't the same be said of the outlines of horses, bison, and oxen that have decorated cave walls for millennia?

Picasso also said, "Art is the lie that enables us to realize the truth." He means that the purpose of art is not simply to decorate a wall. We should see through the work of art, through the image or "lie," to the truth behind it, inside of it. Picasso probably would have recognized a kindred spirit in the earliest artists, who painted the walls of dark, damp caves by torchlight.

ART HISTORY and HISTORIC ART

Cave paintings are the oldest form of art that still exists today. These images were made by painters who held their hand against a wall and blew paint through a hollow reed over it, leaving just the outline instead of a handprint. Most of these paintings seem to be of female hands. In fact, according to a study published by archaeologist Dean Snow in 2015, aeound 75 percent of handprints could be made by female artists now. We don't know much about who made cave art, but we do know that these earliest artists left traces of themselves that have survived for centuries.

Maros-Pangkep Caves

Cave paintings have been found on every continent (except for uninhabited Antarctica), indicating that if humans lived in a place, they were bound to make art there. The oldest cave paintings we have discovered may be those in the Maros-Pangkep Caves in Sulawesi, Indonesia, which were made during the last Ice Age. These cave paintings are almost forty thousand years old.

Experts used to think that humans who migrated from Africa to Europe seventy thousand years ago were the first cave artists. According to this theory, they painted as a way to mark their territory—a warning to the native inhabitants to stay away. Now, because the caves in Indonesia are at least as old as the oldest European cave art—if not older— we know that the Europeans were not the first to come up with the idea. Humans living in Asia were making art as well, and that art was not born from a specific competition with Neanderthals, but from a universal human instinct.

As some of the oldest cave paintings, the paintings of Sulawesi are a window into the life of early man. Using red and deep berry-colored pigments, artists made hand stencils and images of small pigs and deer native to the region. The images of hands are ghostly, and some seem to be missing fingers. Several are handprints, created by dipping a hand in pigment then placing it against the cave wall. This oldest art was painted on the rock ceiling or high up on cave walls, indicating that they were not created idly or without a purpose. Ancient people would have had to use ladders or other structures to reach these parts of the cave to create their paintings.

But great mystery surrounds these works. Though scholars have theories about the paintings' purpose, we'll never know for sure.

Cave of Swimmers

An aristocratic Hungarian who was a race-car driving German spy may not be who you think of when you think of cave paintings. But László Almásy was an adventurer of many trades. In 1926, after he served as a pilot for the Hungarian army in World War I, he raced cars, and he subsequently took one of his cars on an expedition along the Nile, falling in love with the region. He continued to return to the area, making maps and—with partners—searching for the mythic oasis city of Zerzura. He never found Zerzura, but in 1933 he did find the Cave of Swimmers, in the southwest of Egypt near the border with Libya, one of the driest spots in the world. The tracks from his expedition can still be seen in the red sand there.

These cave paintings are between ten thousand and seven thousand years old and depict giraffes, cows, and humans. Many of the humans seem to be floating or swimming, but for many years this mystified researchers. Though the area was certainly greener during the time when the paintings were made, they had found no evidence that there were any bodies of water large enough for swimming. Some thought that the "swimming" figures

Floating on the walls of the Cave of Swimmers, these ghostlike bodies were painted nearly eight thousand years ago and were discovered in the 1930s.

could actually be images of the dead lying on their backs or floating into the afterlife. More recent research has revealed that there may indeed have been lakes near the caves. At the very least, these paintings show us how much our world has changed in the years since these artists made their work. The world they painted, full of lush life and large beasts, seems hard to imagine when we look at images of the dry, dry desert surrounding the Cave of Swimmers.

Lascaux

The caves at Lascaux, France, may be the most famous example of cave paintings that exist today. The art is estimated to be seventeen thousand years old, created during the Paleolithic era. Over two thousand images of horses, deer, humans, aurochs, and even a rhinoceros appear on its walls. The Hall of Bulls, painted with horses, bulls, and stags, is the most famous area of the Lascaux caves because of the impressive size of the animals and sense of motion that the ancient artists captured. The largest bull is 17 feet (5 meters) long, looming over the viewer, and is the largest cave-art animal found to date. Many of the animals are shown in motion, either through the many legs painted on the animals, or through the repetition and overlapping of figures.

But while we discuss the technical side of these paintings, we might forget the beauty of this early art. These painters took images from their daily lives—horses, bulls, hands—and made something breathtaking. The paintings are sophisticated, but the painters responsible probably didn't paint them just to show off new techniques. Instead, visual techniques are tools to serve the artistic vision of the painter.

This series of paintings is different from other early paintings because of the visual perspective shown in some of the images. The Crossed Bison painting is one example. We usually think of perspective in painting as a later development in art, perhaps during the Renaissance, but these works prove that prehistoric man was also interested in showing depth and perspective. The two bison are painted in a niche, with their heads pointing away from each other and their rear legs overlapping, creating a **foreground** and background. Because the heads and torsos of the animals are clearly larger than their hindquarters, they seem like that are charging out at the viewer. This is an impressive display of the artist's mastery of **foreshortening** and perspective. And this technique to represent perspective—pictorial "tricks" to solve the problem on representing three-dimensional forms on a two-dimensional flat surface—is the first in a long chain of such developments, stretching to the Renaissance and beyond.

MATERIALS, TECHNIQUE, and TOOLS

So while we may think of prehistoric man as bumbling or backwards, it turns out that perspective techniques used in cave art came before those used by some of the European masters. Renaissance artist Leonardo da Vinci used paint that had been lightened for faraway objects. Called **sfumato**, artists use this technique in order to create the illusion of distance. For example, in a landscape painting, mountains that line the horizon appear faraway because they are lighter than the mountains in the foreground. Prehistoric artists would make the hindquarters of animals lighter to make it seem like they were charging at the viewer, a simpler form of what Leonardo later perfected. **Chiaroscuro**, or using light and dark pigments to shade a drawing to make it look three-dimensional, is another technique that began in the Renaissance and is still essential to realistic art today.

The fifteenth-century painter, sculptor, and architect Filippo Brunelleschi greatly advanced the understanding of **linear perspective**. Using mathematics and his observations, he made a painting of a building on a piece of glass that was so similar to its subject that all the edges and lines exactly matched up when you looked at the painting held in front of the actual building. This idea of linear perspective—that objects recede and grow smaller in the distance, with exact mathematical rules behind the technique—may even have been pioneered in a less exact way by cave artists. The Crossed Bison with their large heads and chests and smaller hindquarters show this. Perhaps these prehistoric painters noticed how, for example, trees that are far away appear tiny to the human eye, and they decided to include this in their work, using a kind of linear perspective to paint their bison.

The painters of these three examples of cave art used **ochre**—a pigment that ranges from yellow to reddish brown—to paint their art. Yellow ochre pigments get their color from hydrated iron oxide, or limonite, a mineral naturally occurring all over the world. Red ochre is colored by dehydrated iron oxide, or hematite. Ancient people would crush these minerals into a fine powder, then mix them with water or animal fat to make paint. Painters still use these ochres today—any art supply store will have tubes of red and yellow ochre paint that you can purchase. Today we tend to mix the ochre pigment with a plastic, as in acrylic paint, or linseed oil, as in oil paints.

Charcoal was also sometimes used for the deep black color it leaves on the walls. Just like ochres, we still use charcoal in art today. It is the preferred medium for many artists as they sketch subjects. It lends itself to blending, and its rich pigmentation makes charcoal ideal for sketching.

THE MOTIVATIONS OF ANCIENT ARTISTS

Experts still debate the purpose of cave paintings. Some think that they were a sign of power meant to immortalize a particularly successful hunt. This might be supported by the fact that many cave paintings, including the ones at Lascaux, were maintained by the cultures that painted them. Early painters touched up and repainted the works—some over thousands of years—as they aged. This seems like an action motivated by a desire to preserve a cultural memory. Or perhaps this repainting shows that the process of creating the art was more important than the final product.

This idea that process of painting cave art was most important leads many researchers to say that the art had a religious or **shamanistic** function. Also, the locations of a large proportion of the cave art we have discovered—deep in caves that would have been complicated to access by only torchlight, where no one lived—suggests that the art wasn't meant to be viewed every day. Shamanistic hunter-gatherer societies believe that there are many worlds, and they identify "soft spots" between this world and another. These deep caves could have been viewed as such places. Perhaps shamans would journey into the earth and paint these works in a kind of trance, either to call spirits from the other world to ensure the success of a future hunt, or to communicate somehow with the other world. Maybe in the act of painting these figures and by capturing their likeness, the artists felt they gained a sort of power over the physical world. Or in painting an animal, the shaman was thought to cross into the animal world and influence the herd's patterns or fertility.

The Crossed Bison found in the caves
at Lascaux

Cave painters seem to have used a variety tools to apply this pigment to cave walls, but very seldom did they use anything we would recognize as a paintbrush. They used their hands to mask certain areas and blew pigment through a hollow bone around the hand. This resulted in an application of color that allowed for shading, depending on how much paint was blown through the tube. It also appears that they used pads or hands to gently blot paint onto the walls. Thus, cave painting is less concerned with the brushstroke or line, and more concerned with forming shapes. The fluid and expressive shapes of the animals and humans they painted show that this technique that we might consider "simple" was actually used to create complex art.

FINDING MEANING

Many of the caves we know of today are painted with symbols as well as animals and humans. The meaning of these symbols is also unknown. Some think that the dots arranged across the cave walls at Lascaux are an ancient star map, corresponding to constellations that would have shone across the prehistoric sky. Others think the symbols are part of a coming-of-age rite. Yer different scholars believe that they are another part of the religious function of the caves. These experts think the paintings indicate the artist's power over the images he or she created. With all of these possibilities, one thing is clear: early artists show a deep understanding of artistic techniques. They used the environment to their advantage, too.

Visual art is a type of universal language; it crosses cultures and time. We will probably never be sure why these ancient artists created these paintings, and this mystery adds to their intrigue. We can look at ancient pictures on the cave walls and, even though we don't speak the same language or come from the same place and time, understand that the painted image of an animal with four legs, horns, a round head, and a tail is a bison. Images are part of the human experience. Ancient images of animals and early humans found on cave walls prove that we were painting before we had even developed language—we communicated with visual art before we communicated with speech. And even once we developed language and learned how to write, images still played an important part in human communication.

Even if we can't shake the artists' hands, perhaps still dyed with pigment from creating one of these masterworks, and tell them about the beauty and power these images still have, we can at least imagine them— these artists, our ancestors. Who were they? What did they love? And why did they leave us paintings of surprising and haunting power? It's possible that in this case, the questions are more beautiful than the answers. The questions lead us to reflect about ourselves, and how the human spirit has evolved and endured.

The Sphinx and the Pyramids at Giza are among the oldest and best-known monuments in the world.

CHAPTER 2
Early Sculpture

Human figures are relatively rare in prehistoric cave paintings, and those that are depicted are simplified. But another type of art from the prehistoric age is concerned with the human image—specifically the female image. Ancient artists used mammoth ivory, rock, clay, or bone to carve elaborate **Venus figurines**, or small representations of the female form.

In fact, civilizations all over the world paid tribute to their deities by making sculptures. In ancient times, statues of deities were often depicted as humanlike. Small carved objects, believed to ensure safe passage to the afterlife, decorated the tombs of the dead. Large, life-size sculptures of gods, meant to represent their power and beauty, were erected in public spaces. For people in ancient Egypt, death was not the end of life; rather, it was a way to the afterlife. During this time, sculpture was spiritual. Most famously, the great pyramids that served as tombs were a way to show power and magnificence. Though they were smaller in size, the sacred statues that decorated these tombs also held great spiritual power. On these sculptures, the image of the face looks directly ahead, or is forward facing, a perspective technique that was commonly used in prehistoric and ancient depictions of deities.

Olmec Sculpture

The area we know today as Mexico was home to a group of people called the Olmecs from 1500 BCE to 400 BCE. While scholars are still puzzled over why the civilization had completely disappeared by the turn of the millennium, the thousands of pieces of Olmec artwork that survive today have given us a small understanding of how these ancient people spent their time when they were alive.

The most famous Olmec sculptures, known as the "colossal heads," are large stones that had been carved by hand, using hardwood tools, cords, water, and sand, to resemble the faces of gods and goddesses. The heads were lifelike and carefully styled, usually with feathers, headdresses, and animal features (fangs, for example). Though they were decorated, these monuments served more than a decorative purpose; they were used in religious ceremonies and rituals. Art historians believe the serious facial expression of the colossal heads is a representation of ideal beauty and strength. The Olmec sculptures are one of the earliest examples of art that represented beauty and strength as divine attributes—a very common theme throughout art history.

Buddha

Around the time of the collapse of the Olmec civilization, half a world away lived Siddhartha Gautama, the figure we know today as the Buddha. Siddhartha was a wealthy prince, and his father tried to shield him from all pain and suffering. But when one day he finally left the palace walls to see his people, he discovered sickness, old age, suffering, pain, and death. This experience so moved him that he gave up his wealth and traveled the land, trying different ways to seek truth. After a number of experiences, he began to teach the Middle Way, a code for living that preached

Dating back to 1500 BCE, these Olmec sculptures portray deities who have human features.

THE POWER OF PREHISTORIC WOMEN

The oldest sculpture of a human being we have found to date is the Venus of Hohle Fels, named for the German cave where the figure was unearthed. The piece dates to forty thousand years ago, so it is from the same era as the Maros-Pangkep cave art. Carved from mammoth ivory and roughly 2.5 inches (6.4 cm) tall, the proportions of the sculpture emphasize the subject's fertility by enlarging her features associated with reproduction. Alternatively, some researchers suggest that these figurines may represent the actual body types of prehistoric women, who through genetics and nutritional stress could have had bodies shaped much like those of the Venus figurines. Instead of a head, the sculpture has a ring, probably so it could be suspended on a string and worn as a pendant. Experts guess that figurines like this were associated with fertility rites or the work of shamans.

Others, like professor Helen Benigni, see that these figurines were found across a wide area and conclude that they were depictions of a mother goddess or female creator. While many look at the exaggeration of the features of the female body in these figurines and see an objectification of women in ancient times, researchers like Benigni take a different perspective. She says these images point not to the powerlessness of women but to their power. Some have even said that these figurines were self-portraits by female artists. While this idea is widely debated, it is important to note these different ideas about the Venus figurines.

moderation, meditation, and acceptance of suffering. The Buddha, meditating under a bodhi tree, was said to have reach enlightenment after forty-nine days. **Nirvana** is seen as accepting the cycles of death, suffering, and rebirth, and even becoming part of that cycle. Though Buddhism took hold first in India, it eventually spread to China and Japan and began to fade in its native land. Now, there are far fewer Buddhists in India than these other cultures. But Buddhism is still important in India, and Indian Buddhist sculpture remains as a significant art form.

Originally, Indian sculpture did not represent the physical form of the Buddha but showed him through absence—an empty seat, a pair of footprints. But in the first century BCE, artists began depicting the Buddha himself. Their work, called Gandharan after the region where it started, mixed in elements of the **Hellenistic** tradition of sculpture. Some of these elements included long, lithe limbs, closely curled hair, folds of cloth resembling a toga. This version of the Buddha was generally youthful, thin, and graceful. In the later "Golden Age" of the Buddha in India, his curls were stylized until they look like knots on his head, the folds of his robe became stringlike, and he was generally depicted seated and serious. The bun on the top of his head was actually part of his brain, showing how he had reached enlightenment.

Smaller metal images from this period are the ones that traders and pilgrims brought with them on the Silk Road to China, so the Chinese and Japanese interpretations of the Buddha come from this version. These Buddhas were serene, simple, and made gestures, like a hand touching the ground, or fingers held in a pose. These gestures were meant to evoke certain meanings and remind Buddhists of different qualities that the Buddha represented.

Sculptures of Siddhartha are a major part of the Buddhist practice.

As Buddhism evolved, it began to involve a larger cast of characters. There were **bodhisattvas** who served the Buddha, and many other guardians and minor figures. The statues were used as part of the *mikkyo* practice of Buddhism. The statues were mostly produced in Nepal, made of metal and painted with exquisite colors. Buddhist sculpture gives us an insight into the cultures where Buddhism spread. Each society reinterpreted the Buddha, and his depiction, to fit their own cultural background and needs. Unlike, for example, crucifixes, which are largely similar in style and form across cultures and centuries, sculptures of the Buddha evolved and changed to fit the culture around them. Chinese Buddhas look distinct from Indian or Korean Buddhas. Art was a tool of culture, not something defined by a central seat of power, unlike Christian art, which for many centuries stemmed directly from conventions set by the Catholic Church.

GREEK CLASSICISM

Greek sculpture was a spiritual medium during the **Archaic period**, which spanned the seventh and sixth centuries BCE. Standing sculptures of divine entities were placed at temple entrances. These statutes, often adorned with clothing, were meant to be lifelike; if the sculpture seemed real, then its power was also real. Sculptors also created figures of young men (**kouroi**) and young women (**korai**) that served as symbols of gods and goddesses.

In Greece, during the fifth and fourth centuries BCE, famous thinkers like Plato and Socrates were thinking about the laws of nature and man and using reason as a way to find truth in these great unknowns. Classical artists, scientists, and philosophers from this time used reason in pursuit of ideal beauty. Greece experienced a period of rapid cultural growth. In fact, many of the political, artistic, and philosophical ideas from this time shaped Western civilization.

We know the primary purpose of art from the ancient past was to communicate with the spiritual world—gods and goddesses often took human form. During the classical period, this was no longer the case. The classical artist aspired to re-create life in the most accurate way possible, creating a sense of permanence, clarity, and harmony. **Heroic realism**, a realistic portrayal of the human body, showed extraordinary beauty or someone in a significant (usually triumphant) moment. Heroic realism brought about new types of sculpture: portraits or busts of rulers as a sign of power and strength, victory sculptures that depict a battle scene, and the torso.

Perfection and Polyclitus

What makes something beautiful? Our perception of beauty varies based on cultural standards and personal experience. One person watches the sun set with fascination; another sees nothing special. Put simply, *beauty is in the eye of the beholder.* But what if the beholder is a film critic and beauty is defined by the mastery of cinematic techniques? In this case, beauty is determined by an intellectual response instead of an emotional one. If beauty is objective, then artists should aspire to create perfect beauty, or **beau ideal**, in their work. Many of our contemporary ideas about beauty come from the classical interpretation of beau ideal. While classical sculptures of the male form do not come with sunglasses and a varsity letter, our ideas about the stereotypical high school jock are directly linked to classical ideals. Typically athletic and handsome, the jock is a symbol for popularity, masculinity—the epitome of cool.

In art, athleticism has been associated with masculinity since at least the fifth century BCE, when the sculptor

Polyclitus discovered that the ideal male physique could be created using proportion. This was a huge change. Before the classical period, "perfection" was an abstract concept, a heavenly ideal that humans could never achieve. According to Polyclitus's theory, perfection was a mathematical equation rather than a personal expression.

None of Polyclitus's original sculptures survive because they were made of bronze and were likely melted and repurposed for weapons and armor during times of war. A full transcript of the original text of his treatise is also missing. Yet Polyclitus's legacy lives on. Many sculptors copied his work, and Greek historians described his work. The calculations outlined in his writing were quickly accepted as standard for sculpting the perfect human form and remained in use for hundreds of years. In his famous first-century-CE text, *Natural History*, Pliny says,

Polyclitus's *Doryphoros* represents the beau ideal because it depicts man in perfect proportion.

> Polyclitus of Sicyon, a pupil of Hageladas, made a "Diadoumenus," a supple youth, famous for having cost 100 talents, and a "Doryphorus," a virile-looking boy. He also made a statue that artists

call the "Canon," and from which they derive the principles of their art, as if from a law of some kind, and he alone of men is deemed to have rendered art itself in a work of art."

Today, the ancient *Diadumenus* and *Doryphoros* marble statues that survive are replicas of Polyclitus's original sculptures—models of the "perfect" sculpture he described. The *Diadumenus* and *Doryphoros* statues both depict young athletic males—one is wearing a diadem, or a headband worn as a symbol of victory; the other has a spear on his shoulder, prepared for athletic contest. The statues represent the ideal male: competitive, strong, young, and victorious. Polyclitus finds his sculpture "perfect" or beautiful in part because of its symmetrical patterns, or "opposing responses." Humans tend to instinctively prefer symmetrical objects to asymmetrical ones, even if we aren't always aware of it. Though beauty is not a form of absolute truth that brings us all together, it is, however, part of our nature to seek out symmetry.

Yet a description from the Louvre Museum reminds us that we should not compare ourselves to Polyclitus's work or seek the symmetry he presents in ourselves. His ideal form cannot actually be achieved by humans:

> However natural his pose may appear, the Diadumenus should not therefore be viewed as the representation of any individual athlete savoring his victory. It is rather the result of rigorous intellectual research, which finds its three-dimensional expression in this idealized, rigorously considered anatomy. This physique created through mathematical calculation renders the Diadumenus the ideal, and not the portrait, of an athlete, and places him definitively in a world beyond our own.

Perhaps Polyclitus tells us a much bigger story about the power of art. We already know that, before Polyclitus's time, sculptures of gods and goddesses had faces, bodies, or other characteristics that resembled the human image. We also know that they had nonhuman attributes—an extravagant headpiece, a body with feathers, or the claws of a predator—that communicated their other-worldliness. The sculpture itself had spiritual power. This was true for Polyclitus's sculptures too, but instead of being objects of spirituality, they were objects that *represented* spirituality through the mathematical process behind them. For classical artists, achieving perfection was a way to reach the divine. Of course, it is impossible to achieve the standard of beauty that ancient sculptors represented in these works. Again, attainment of beauty ideals was aside from the point. Rather, sculptors tried to connect with the divine on the terms defined by their cultures. It's amazing to think how often mathematics and science were a key part of this process. Sculpture as a medium serves as a powerful reminder of the link between the arts and the sciences.

In the next chapter, we'll see how artists used a new innovation, the sketchbook, to push the boundaries of human representation even further. The artists we'll discuss also demonstrate the complex relationship between art and innovations of all kinds.

Leonardo da Vinci's most famous sketch is the *Vitruvian Man*.

CHAPTER 3
The Sketchbook

The term "renaissance" comes from the French for "rebirth" and is famously used to describe the period of artistic development and scientific discovery in Europe that took place from the fourteenth to the seventeenth century. What we now refer to as the Early Modern Age actually began long before the 1400s—the idea that beauty and truth could be attained through reason dates back to Greece's classical era. Artists from the Renaissance revisited the classical idea that beauty was a function of technique. These Renaissance artists wanted to portray the world as realistically as possible. The idea of the perfect form was reborn. Remember Polyclitus's belief that the perfect sculpture was an accurate representation of man's perfect form? For the Renaissance artist, the perfect sculpture was an accurate representation of man's *actual* form.

While the Renaissance was a renewal of classical ideals, it was also a period of invention and innovation. The "rebirth" wasn't just an update to an older culture, but essentially a new movement. Leonardo da Vinci's sketchbooks demonstrate this. He drew and redrew forms, researching, improving, and seeking this new kind of perfection and harmony. The sketchbook's relatively low cost and its compact size made it an important tool for an artist whose goal was to make art that was not just beautiful

but also accurate, true to life, and true to experience—
a process that requires many drafts.

TYPES of SKETCHING

Leafing through the pages of Leonardo's notebooks, you'd
see drawings for an anemometer (an instrument that
measures the speed of the wind), a flying machine, a giant
crossbow, a scuba suit, and more, but one of Leonardo's
most important inventions won't be found sketched out
there. That invention is the sketchbook itself. Paper was still

LEONARDO DA VINCI

One of the most famous painters and Renaissance men
wasn't born to a lord or an artist, but to unmarried peasant
parents in the small Italian town of Vinci. Leonardo da Vinci
was apprenticed as a young boy to a famous Florentine
painter, and there he studied the art and craft of painting.
Despite his wide-ranging fame today, only about fifteen of his
paintings survive, including *The Last Supper* and *The Mona
Lisa*. The bulk of Leonardo's work that still exists is in his
notebooks. While he is primarily remembered as a painter, he
saw himself as an expert in many fields. He was a scientist,
researcher, and inventor, and many credit him with inventing
the helicopter, the parachute, tanks, and maybe even an
early calculator. But his sketchbooks weren't published in
his time, and so most of today's inventions that are similar to
ones imagined by Leonardo don't directly trace back to his
work, since technology was not advanced enough at his time
to bring his inventions to life. For a long time, Leonardo's
innovations lived only in the pages of his books.

new to Europe, and Leonardo was one of the first artists to take advantage of the inexpensive and durable alternative to parchment. Before paper, the concept of a sketchbook was unimaginable, wasteful.

Leonardo's passion for art and science were intertwined, and we can see in his sketchbooks how his studies for paintings and his inspired inventions were produced with the same exacting eye. He saw the human body as a metaphor for the rules of the universe, and he believed that everything was connected through scientific principles. The *Vitruvian Man* exemplifies this idea. Leonardo drew a man in two positions constrained in a circle to illustrate how mathematical principles of geometry can be applied to the human body. In his sketches, we can see how Leonardo saw the world: a complex system of relationships between humans and the laws of the natural world. Leonardo drew the *Vitruvian Man* using everything in he knew— his knowledge of the human form, of mathematics, and of perspective—but the place he drew it was on a page in his notebook. Thus, the sketchbook is both a physical object and a space to experiment with concepts. The object itself—blank pages bound together between covers—wasn't invented by Leonardo. However, the use of the space to *think* visually, to work out ideas and form systems, to revise and re-create, was pioneered by him.

You probably know drafting and revision as parts of the writing process, but they apply to the visual arts as well. For example, a painter can experiment with perspective just like a novelist can revise a draft of his or her story so that it is told from a different character's point of view. In fact, the term "revise" applies perfectly here: the painter refines the work after finding ways to *re-see* the subject. The visual artist's sketchbook is a record of this revision process. We'll look at three different types of sketches that famous visual artists have used to prepare their masterpieces.

Scientific Illustration

The Renaissance's drive to make the unknown known spurred artists, researchers, and scientists to create detailed sketchbooks whose purpose was not to plan for a large painting or study how to draw a model's certain pose, but to exist as a final product themselves. Conrad Gesner, a scientist and near contemporary of Leonardo, used sketchbooks to document plants he collected. His unfinished work *Historia plantarum* includes 1,500 detailed, labeled drawings of plants. Gesner was a physician, and his study of plants was for medicinal purposes. His sketchbooks represent another use of the form. Instead of searching for the divine order in nature and inventing new objects as Leonardo did, Gesner used his sketchbooks to document and define rare botanical specimens. Also unlike Leonardo, Gesner did not keep his books secret; he would write to friends and colleagues and ask that they send him a catalog of all the plants they knew in their area, and if they listed one he had never heard of, he would ask that they send a specimen for him to study and sketch. If they couldn't send him a seed or plant, he would commission four different artists to go sketch the plant, then he would take those four drawings and make his own based off those. He would reward those who found a new plant by naming it after them. In this way, he used a network of botanists and enthusiasts who would all exchange their work and help each other.

In the era before photographs, sketches like these were the closest one could come to accurate documentation. Gesner's sketching process shows that he saw his drawings as more than simple depictions of plants. They are images that become more than just reproductions of nature; these images both depict the object and replace it. The botanist could study Gesner's sketches to learn about the anatomy of a plant without ever seeing the plant in real life. In this way, the sketch replaces the plant. (Of course, scientific illustrations are used by painters, sculptors, and other visual artists, too.) The specimen itself is no longer necessary, and the image becomes the definition of what the plant should be. The drawing, and not the plant, is the official standard.

Croquis

Often called the "Prince of Painting," the painter Raphael is known for his masterpieces in portraiture and the large colorful frescoes of Madonna that decorated the Palace of the Vatican. In order to create these timeless works of art, Raphael practiced drawing techniques. Before dipping a brush in a pool of paint, he took red chalk and drew models of human subjects on paper. For Raphael, revision was mostly refining his technique, a way to learn how to compose an image through drafting and redrafting a leg or a face until he felt he had achieved perfection. He then used this composition for his final painting. His sketches are as historically important as his finished paintings, and many of them are on display in galleries along with finished works of art. From his sketches, art historians have a better understanding of the creative process. For example, the early drafts of Raphael's painting *Saint Catherine of Alexandria* can be seen at the Ashmolean Museum in Oxford. In *Study for Saint Catherine*, we can see that the portrait began as a full-length drawing. Raphael then sketches out four versions of Saint Catherine, this time drawing three-quarters of her body instead of her full body. On one page, her face appears, bodiless, like an apparition.

Sketches of the human form in different positions that function as templates—the basic shape and outline adapted by other artists—are called croquis. In a way, a croquis sketch is a way to stop motion so that the artist can make a still image from a world of ever-changing scenery. Perhaps this is what makes *Saint Catherine of Alexandria*, the

During the Renaissance, extremely detailed drawings of plants, seeds, and the human body played a critical role in scientific discovery.

Madonna series, and Raphael's other portraits so timeless. He searched for the "humanness" of the human form, and he found it—or, perhaps more accurately, he created it. He would sketch several drafts, until he had composed what he believed to be the most human image, what remained true across time and place. Once composed, croquis are then spread around the art world—today, fashion designers sketch croquis from live models, and digital illustration programs provide body templates.

Pochade

While a croquis is a quick line drawing, a pochade is a study that uses color. Artists would take small boxes of paints and an easel outside to paint *plein air*, or "open air." These sketches were generally small and quickly executed, as the point was to complete a study of the colors in a scene before the weather or light changed. Pochades were impractical for much of oil painting's history because until the mid-1800s the best storage container painters had for their paints was a pig's bladder. The artists would grind their pigments finely, mix them with oil, and then fill these bladders with the colors to keep them from drying out. Then, when a color was needed, the painter would prick the bladder and squeeze the paint out. This was an impractical tool to carry outside, though, because the bladders would easily burst. Also, there was no foolproof method for sealing up the hole. When the metal paint tube was invented, artists were freed from their studios and could venture out of doors to paint quick, immediate scenes from life. It's no coincidence that the invention of the paint tube coincides with the beginning of impressionist art.

Before impressionism, pochades were used by artists to study the colors of a church in the setting sun or the glint of light off a sweaty horse's back, but these were just that, studies. They would be brought back to the studio and used as resources as the artist created a larger, more formal work. So these sketches were not a final product but a way of visual planning for a larger piece, using color instead of line. Impressionists took these color sketches and made them the art itself. Equipped with folding easels, small prepped canvases, and their shiny metal tubes of paint, they would hike into fields or paint in parks, gardens, town squares, or cafés. Their works were **gestural**, and color and immediacy were the most important elements of the work.

Raphael's sketch of St. Catherine

Many artists would spend no longer than an hour or so on a painting. Their pochades were their finished pieces. Claude Monet is an excellent example of this. He painted scenes over and over in different lights and seasons: his garden and water lilies, churches, homes, and most prominently, the Rouen Cathedral. He made twenty pochades of the cathedral at different times of day, trying to capture the different qualities of light at certain hours. He would then rework and polish those pochades in his studio. By keeping the subject the same and varying the time and techniques of painting, this series becomes a portrait of light itself—its shifting, subtle, and transformative powers.

Another important difference between the paintings of the impressionists and the work of earlier artists was the color of the background the artist worked on. Traditionally, painters would lay a dark ground for their work, painting the canvas a deep brown or even black, then they would add lights and darks to bring out shapes and forms. This way of painting can be compared to sculpture. The artist added and subtracted until the form was carved out of the background. But, like the blank pages in a sketchbook, pochades were generally made on small, thin, white or neutral canvases. The blankness of the page or these small canvases positions the artist as the creator, bringing a world into being from nothing, from blankness. In this way, artists like Monet who used these color sketches were more like photographers; they used their eye as the lens, their hand as the camera, the white canvas as their undeveloped film. It was as close to an instantaneous image as painting could allow.

NEW VISIONS

The sketchbook is both a space of imagination and reality. "Visualize" is a word with two meanings: to imagine and to make visible. Sketchbooks allowed artists like Leonardo

For artists like Monet, the sketchbook was a place to study color.

Monet painted the Rouen Cathedral twenty times, adjusting the shades of paint to match differing qualities of light.

Leonardo completed this drawing in 1503. It demonstrates the myriad ways he used sketchbooks to record his inventions and develop his art.

to visualize the world. Unlike ancient artists, Renaissance artists were driven by a suspicion that there was an unseen order or divinity in what we see, in objects and people. If cave painters thought their art was a window into a spirit world and the Olmecs' sculptures were representations of the divine in a human form, these artists sought to use their skills to uncover how the perfection of divinity ran throughout everything in the physical world. Aware of the spiritual nature that ran through all forms of his work, Leonardo da Vinci said, "O powerful action! What spirit can penetrate your nature? What tongue will know how to

express that marvel? None, for sure. That is where human discourse turns to the contemplation of the divine."
The sketchbook can thus be seen as a way for artists to make their thoughts visible on the page. The sketchbook becomes a world of the artists' making, where they were creators and experimenters.

American photographer Ansel Adams
(1902–1984)

CHAPTER 4
Photography

During the Renaissance, artists and scientists were more similar than different. Often, as in the case of Leonardo da Vinci, the artist and the scientist were one and the same. Leonardo believed the parts inside of our bodies could be known, and he researched the body by studying cadavers. From his scientific investigation, we have some of the earliest surviving concepts of human anatomy. From his skillfully drawn illustrations, we can see the insides of our bodies. Yet with an X-ray, the real image of our bones replaces Leonardo's illustrations, and we see ourselves in a new way.

Photography can also be considered a method of travel. We can take a "trip" to the Grand Canyon; we can see its breathtaking views without packing up the car and taking a vacation. Aerial photography replaces the maps that were once clumsily sketched out by explorers. Because of cameras, we know more than ever about our world.

The camera, in its most primitive form, is nothing like the device we know today. You couldn't carry a camera in your pocket; it didn't have features like automatic flash or a button that allowed you to zoom in or out. In fact, the prototype of the camera is called a **pinhole camera**, and it could not even produce a permanent replica of the image on another surface. Conceptualized during the fifth century BCE, the pinhole camera predates photography. Using a small hole in a box that had been painted black on all four sides, a group of Chinese philosophers, known as the **Mohists**, discovered that light rays from an object that entered the box through the hole, or an **aperture**, projected an upside-down image on its opposite side. It may be hard to believe, but this box evolved over the centuries into the cameras we know today.

There have been so many major innovations throughout the history of photography. The **camera obscura**, the **daguerreotype**, and the **Kodak camera** are just three monumental developments out of many. For example, between 1826 and 1861, at least seven different

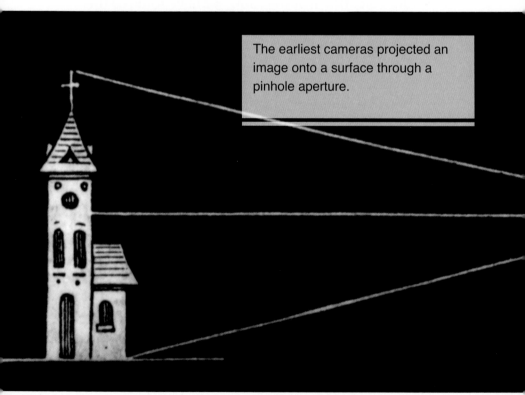

The earliest cameras projected an image onto a surface through a pinhole aperture.

men experimented with various light-sensitive chemicals and surfaces that could hold images. Their scientific approach—trial and error—led to seven different methods of developing photographs. And these are just the innovations in one area of photography.

The CAMERA OBSCURA and the CHEMIST

Historians attribute the innovation of the camera obscura to an Egyptian inventor, Alhazen, who lived from the mid-tenth to the early eleventh century CE. He was also a physicist, and he used the camera obscura to observe solar eclipses. The major difference between the camera obscura and the pinhole camera is that the

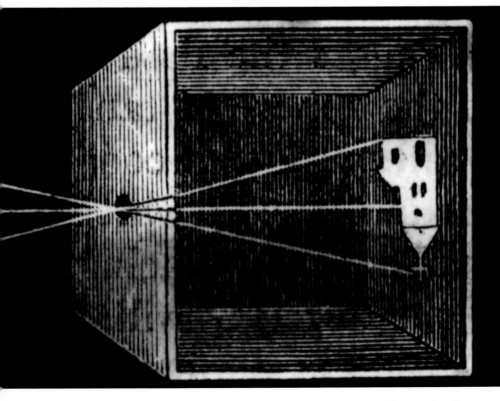

image created by Alhazen's device is projected onto a wall or screen instead of inside the camera itself. Otherwise, the two are almost identical; both use a light that enters through a small aperture to project an image in a dark space. The camera obscura could project large, wall-sized images onto an external space. The camera obscura varied in size: it could be a small box, just like the pinhole camera, or it could be room-sized. For the larger versions, viewers entered a dark room to see the projected images. In fact, "camera obscura" is Latin for "darkened chamber."

The device was used as a drawing aid—artists traced the projected image onto paper—until the 1820s, when French inventor and scientist Joseph-Nicéphore Niépce successfully produced the first permanently fixed image, using a metal plate that has been coated with a type of asphalt called **bitumen of Judea**. When the plate was exposed to sun, the bitumen hardened. After being rinsed with lavender oil, the plate contained an etched replica of the image. Niépce produced the first photograph: a permanent image that was produced using light and light-sensitive materials. It seems fitting that the word "photography" means "drawing with light" in Greek.

Joseph-Nicéphore Niépce spent nearly a decade experimenting with different materials, in search of a way to produce a permanent image. Upon finding it, he became a revolutionary figure in art history: the inventor of photography. For Niépce, however, this was not the end of his work in the field. Instead, he continued to find ways to improve the photographic process. In 1829, he partnered with fellow Frenchman Louis-Jacques-Mandé Daguerre. They signed an agreement, and together, they worked toward perfecting photography.

Niépce died in 1833, and Daguerre continued without his partner. Niépce may not have been alive when Daguerre revealed the daguerreotype, which we will discuss in the following section, but he undoubtedly played a major part in its formation.

DAGUERREOTYPES: PROCESSING LIGHT in a DARK CHAMBER

In the art history and photography worlds, the year 1839 was significant—Louis-Jacques-Mandé Daguerre discovered a new way to produce fixed, or permanent, images. Named after its inventor, the daguerreotype was a metal plate that contained a photographic image. What made Daguerre's invention so important was not the photograph itself; it was how the photograph was made. After years of experimentation with different light-sensitive chemicals and materials, Daguerre perfected his method. To make a daguerreotype, a silver-plated sheet of metal was treated with iodine vapors so that the surface would be light sensitive. Next, the metal plate was placed in a camera where it was exposed to light. An invisible image, also referred to as a **latent image**, became visible when it was developed in mercury fumes. Finally, the plate was rinsed in salt water, making the image permanent.

The method has been credited as the earliest photographic process. A commercial success, the daguerreotype spread quickly and was the most commonly used way to produce photographic images for two decades.

Because of the long exposure time and chemical process that went into producing a daguerreotype, subjects were required to sit still for long periods of time.

The CAMERA THAT CAPTURED the WORLD: KODAK

In 1877, a young man named George Eastman was planning his future in real estate. He worked at the Rochester Savings Bank in Rochester, New York, as a junior bookkeeper and had saved enough money to travel to Hispaniola to begin his career. Eastman's father was the founder of a business school; the entrepreneurial spirit seemed to run in the family blood. As a boy, Eastman's early education took place on the farm where he grew up. Though he attended school when he was eight years old until he was fifteen, he was mostly self-taught, led by his own natural curiosity. A future in land speculation looked promising, but Eastman never made it to Hispaniola. Something much bigger took place: he bought his first camera.

From this point on, he became obsessed with photography, and he initiated an apprenticeship under two local photographers. He resumed his self-directed education by reading the *British Journal of Photography* on a regular basis. Savvy to the contemporary technology in his field, Eastman began to experiment with the plates and chemicals that were used to develop photographs, which had not changed much since Daguerre. In order to advance beyond capturing portraits and landscapes, photographers needed a camera that could capture moving objects and a development process that did not require a "portable" darkroom. In an age of cell phone cameras, the term portable darkroom sounds ridiculous—it's difficult to imagine a time when cameras were too big to fit inside your back pocket or too heavy hang around your neck on an adjustable strap. This is because, in 1884, Eastman introduced dry film, which replaced the chemically treated

DOCUMENTATION OF EPHEMERAL ART

Andy Goldsworthy, a contemporary visual artist, creates site-specific art that is too **ephemeral**, or short lived, and too geographically remote to be viewed by the general public. In his work, he might weave branches together in a forest to create a dome, place red autumn leaves on the ground in a circular pattern, or even use icicles as his medium, linking them together to form an arch or spiral. The role of both nature and time in art are clearly expressed in a series of what Goldsworthy calls "rain shadows." He described the process of making a rain shadow in an NPR interview: "When it rains, I lay down or I find a surface quickly that I think will produce a good rain shadow, and I lay there, and when it's wet enough, I get up and there is left me—my imprint, my shadow." But he's not making the rain shadows for the sake of the statement they make about the ephemerality of art. Above all, Goldsworthy wants his artistic process to deepen his understanding of the world. He says, "The point is not just to make the shadow, it's to understand

the rain that falls and the relationship with rain and the different rhythms of different rainfalls."

These works are not built to last, and the only way that most of us will see them (and other ephemeral art) is through the meticulous photographs Goldsworthy takes of his art.

"It's not about art," Andy Goldsworthy says. "It's just about life and the need to understand that a lot of things in life do not last."

plates that were commonly used up until this time. The dry film was stored in a roll that protected the captured images from light exposure. Roll film technology eliminated the need for photographers to develop their images on-site; in fact, Kodak's mail-in developing service freed them from the process completely.

In 1888, Eastman went down in history as the man who brought photography to mainstream culture. He was the founder of the Kodak company and inventor of its signature camera, the first of its kind that had the ability to hold rolls of film. The Kodak camera was user friendly. Anyone who owned a camera could be a photographer, and when Kodak released the Brownie camera in 1900, anyone with a spare dollar could own a camera. Photography was easy; in fact, Kodak's first slogan was "You press the button, we do the rest." This was only the beginning. Flexible film, color film, the pocket camera, and the aerial camera are just a few of the many innovations that came from Kodak.

Kodak's roll film was revolutionary, making photography accessible to the general public.

The ROLE of the PHOTOGRAPHER

Photography is not only an art form itself, but a tool that aids memory, documents reality, and allows us to see art we could never visit in person. We all know about visual masterpieces, like Leonardo's *Mona Lisa* and Michaelangelo's *David*. We can visualize the works of art even if we've never been to the Louvre or the Galleria dell'Accademia di Firenze. Looking at a photograph can sometimes act as a way to teleport to far-flung places. But photography serves other roles, too: photographers create portraits, landscape art, and even document war.

Photographer as Portraitist

The daguerreotype was revealed to the world in 1839 by Louis Dauguerre, and just three years later, the first professional photography studio was opened by Richard Beard in London. By 1849, one hundred thousand daguerreotype portraits had been made in Paris alone. The photographic portrait was not just for the wealthy or adventurous; almost anyone could afford to have one made. There were some technical difficulties, as the camera was very large and bulky. The subject would have to sit or stand perfectly still for several seconds at least for the long **exposure** time, and the camera was not easily transportable, so studios often had backdrops painted of parks or rowboats to give the impression that the subjects were outdoors. Most of these early portraits were carefully posed, and the subjects seem stiff and formal. As technology advanced and cameras became smaller and more portable, portraits began to be less formal and more fluid.

Another important advance in portrait photography was the ability to print the image onto photographic paper and to reproduce a single negative many times. This way, portraits of leaders, politicans, and celebrities could be reproduced on sturdy cards and distributed widely. Suddenly everyone could know exactly what the president looked like. Portrait photography brought the world closer together. From sweethearts exchanging images before a soldier went off to war to cards with the image of Queen Victoria sold at stands in England, the portrait linked couples, families, and countries together.

Photographer as Landscape Artist

Famous for his photographs of the West and national parks, Ansel Adams considered himself a fine artist, and his work blazed the trail for other artists who used photography as their medium. He captured the landscape with a large-view camera, a painstaking and slow process that produces huge negatives that give great detail and clarity to the resulting images. Many galleries considered photography to be commercial or journalistic—suitable for family snapshots or newspapers, but not the walls of respected museums. Adams and his contemporaries showed the world that photography can be just as labor intensive, controlled, and beautiful as a painting.

Photographer as Photojournalist

Eddie Adams began his career as a photographer in the Korean War, as a Marine Corps combat photographer. As his career progressed, he began to work for the Associated Press, covering a total of thirteen wars. He became an expert and respected photojournalist. Photojournalism is a particular form of photography that aims to be "real," to give a factual report, like a journalist's article would.

Adams's most famous image is *Saigon Execution*. He photographed a Vietnamese general, Nguyen Ngoc Loan, executing a Viet Cong prisoner, Nguyen Van Lem.

He called this a "reflex picture," different from the kind of photograph that is considered and composed by the photographer. He took this photo, rather than made it. Though it was the most famous image in his body of work, he wished he would be remembered for other work that was less damaging and less reflexive. Yet the importance of the image, which helped to turn public sentiment against the Vietnam War, can't be denied.

FRAMING the FUTURE

Photography preserves ephemeral moments: the beauty of a rain shadow is that it is at once fleeting and permanent. A camera captures an image, allowing us to see art before it vanishes in the sun, but it also ruins the ephemerality of the work. Likewise, digital media technology changes our relationship with the art. Now we can easily access a digital image of almost any painting. We can "see" the painting, but we can't fully *experience* it. We can't study the brushstrokes left in the dried paint from all angles, we can't marvel over the scale of the work. Yet part of the beauty of Goldsworthy's rain shadows can't be seen in the photographs—his artistic process, the contemplation he brings to the moment, and the fact that it'll be dried and gone by the afternoon.

Think about the ancient cave painters who valued the experience of creating art more than the final product. Art is at once a personal and universal impulse. Photography offers us an opportunity to appreciate the natural world we inhabit as a work of art. In Goldsworthy, we see an artist free to create beauty simply for the experience of beauty. Art can be a collection of beautiful experiences that hang from the walls of our memory, our own private gallery.

Thanks to CAD technology, architects can see lifelike versions of their designs before breaking ground.

CHAPTER 5
CAD

Even though you might not have a clear sense of what CAD (computer-aided design) does, today it touches virtually every part of our lives, from the toothbrush you use in the morning to the office building down the street to the cartoon you turn on after dinner. But this technology didn't spring up overnight. Ivan Sutherland was a pioneer of this field, beginning in the 1960s. He imagined a virtual reality that was indistinguishable from reality, one that was controlled with a computer that had the power to create:

> The ultimate display would, of course, be a room within which the computer can control the existence of matter. A chair displayed in such a room would be good enough to sit in. Handcuffs displayed in such a room would be confining, and a bullet displayed in such a room would be fatal.

Sutherland's vision was far from the capabilities of computers at the time he envisioned virtual reality. Up until that point, if you wanted to use a computer, you communicated with the computer by inserting punched paper cards that the computer "read," by typing on a keyboard, or by using a system of switches and

IVAN SUTHERLAND: SKETCHING ON A SCREEN

As a young man, Ivan Sutherland was fascinated by computers and had the opportunity to write programs (on punched paper tape) for SIMON, an early computer. While completing his PhD at the Massachusetts Institute of Technology, Sutherland's doctoral thesis was titled, "Sketchpad: A Man-Machine Graphical Communications System" and described his invention, the first graphical user interface. This was before the computer mouse was invented. Sutherland's Sketchpad was a revolutionary interface that allowed you to use a "light pen" stylus to communicate with the computer by pointing and dragging on the screen itself—much like we can tap the screens of our phones today. In Sketchpad, you could use your pen directly on the screen to place points, create lines, drag and drop, expand shapes, and create complex drawings. As a drafting tool, it was important, and as a new way of thinking about human interaction with computers, it was astounding. The idea of creating images on a screen, then being able to manipulate them, was simply unthinkable before Sketchpad. Harry McCracken, a reporter for *Time*, said:

> I asked Sutherland if he knew he was jump-starting a revolution which would go on for decades when he created Sketchpad. "Of course not," he told me. "The future is very hard to see. I had no idea of what would happen in

the future, nor did I think of it much. I just wanted to make nice pictures."

Even an innovator like Sutherland, who continues to do cutting-edge work in the computer science field, did not anticipate the far-reaching effects of his inventions.

Before digital tablets with touch screens, there was the Sketchpad.

buttons. And the computer screen only displayed text or simple objects.

Now, with computer-aided design technology, designers and artists can visualize and manipulate reality, without the usual costs in materials and labor that would be necessary if we didn't have computer programs that could create digital models. While building a scale model of a car body using clay is useful, it is also time consuming, difficult to store, complicated to translate into the computer code used to program production lines, and hard to change or tweak. A computer model can look and seem real, while also allowing greater flexibility. Using CAD technologies, designers, artists and animators can create complex 3D animated or still images that approximate—or even enhance—reality.

CAD TODAY

CAD has two branches: industrial design, and computer-generated art and animation. The industrial design application of CAD allows designers and architects to use computer imaging and graphics to create digital mock-ups of products and buildings, so that instead of having to build a physical model to see what the design will look like, we can now use computer technology to create virtual models. CAD enables architects, engineers, and product designers to model their products accurately, aiding them in both the creation of the design and the selling of the design to the customer. As an industrial design platform, CAD allows architects and planners to create a 3D building model, layer it onto an image of the proposed site, and study where shadows will fall on the building and how it will appear from different angles, for example. And these models—both 2D and 3D—are not just so the viewer can get an idea of how the object will look. Advanced CAD technologies now allow us to test the physical properties of things like buildings and bridges using computers. For example, will this new design for a bridge be strong enough to withstand hurricane-force winds? A CAD model is often one of the first steps to finding out.

There are many different software programs that allow the user to create industrial CAD models. AutoCAD was one of the first to appear on the market, and it is still a leader. There are two ways to use CAD to design an object. Let's take a car as our example. Using 2D CAD technologies, an automotive designer could plan the basic look of the car—how the hood curves and the shapes of the windows, among hundreds of other design choices. In a CAD program, the image is not simply static, as it would be if a designer had drawn it with pencil and paper. Using the computer, the designer can tweak angles, save changes, and set certain mathematical proportions while manipulating others.

The next stage would be creating a 3D CAD image, often called a wireframe model. This is formed from points, lines, arcs, and curves—simple geometric shapes—that are joined together across planes to create a 3D model that can be rotated, resized, and manipulated. From this wireframe model, a designer could add digital layers that give a very realistic rendering of the conceptual car. So without ever lifting a pencil or bending a piece of steel, a car is "made."

The other branch of computer-aided design leads us to computer-generated imagery, or CGI. While "CAD" as a term is usually used in the industrial design context discussed above, CGI is also a form of computer-aided design and a descendant of Sutherland's Sketchpad program. CGI artists use computer programs to create simple "skeletons" of moving characters or objects, much the like wireframes used in industrial CAD. Then the objects are animated, and they can be made to dance or fly their way across our screens. The techniques that designers use to layer a realistic "skin" onto wireframe CAD models is paramount in CGI, where the "skin" characters wear is part of the art of the animation itself. Now the artist's imagination and technical skill are the only limits to the wonders we can see on screen.

From dragons breathing fire to whole cities being destroyed to armies that stretch as far as the eye can see, CGI and CAD have transformed the movie-making industry. The line between what is real and what is fake blurs as live-action movies—even ones you wouldn't expect to use CGI, like dramas—embrace the possibilities that CGI offers to create something more realistic in appearance. For example, the final scene in the movie *Titanic*, in which the main characters Rose and Jack are floating in the freezing-cold ocean after the ship begins to sink, uses CGI prominently. While the actors were in real water, it was a pool on a soundstage, not the open ocean. And the pool was a warm 80 degrees. The white plumes of chilled breath you see from the actors' mouths were added later, using CGI. So at times, CGI allows approximations of reality that surpass even what literal reality could offer; the director could never have made his actors float in near-freezing water for take after take—it wouldn't have been safe. But using CGI, he can create the look of the real thing, without having to ask his actors to experience that reality.

CAD and Other Art Mediums

We can see the connections between CAD models, CGI, and both sculpture and painting. Sculpture is distinct from a two-dimensional art form like painting. Let's take the example of an image of a woman. A painting of this woman opens up a window to another world, where she is represented on the canvas but exists without weight, form, or substance in our world. We can't walk around her, touch her arm, or examine the back of her head. The painting creates a new reality that both invites the viewer in and keeps the viewer out, as the image of the woman is not projected into our world but trapped in the frame.

A sculpture of the same woman functions very differently. Her form—in marble or clay—is part of our reality. We can walk around her, touch her arm (if the museum guards don't catch us), and if we were strong enough, we could lift her form in our arms. This three-dimensional art exists in our reality. The air surrounding the woman is the same air we are standing in. The room the sculpture sits in is the same one we circle. Unlike a two-dimensional painting, the three-dimensional sculptural representation of this woman takes up our space, the space of the viewer, instead of inviting the viewer into another, imagined space, as a painting does.

Since CAD is such a recent tool for creating images, philosophers largely have not trained their attention on how we experience these digital images. But we can see how CAD models and CGI animations have parallels in the older art world. CAD wireframe models seem to digitally approximate sculptures. They can be rotated and viewed in an approximation of three-dimensional space, and their purpose is to imagine how an object would look in our reality—how a concept car would look from all angles—not to create a new reality, as paintings do. But in a twenty-first century twist, the three dimensional has been collapsed into a two-dimensional screen. A CAD wireframe model is almost a sculpture in another reality. On the other hand, CGI animations and images are more similar to paintings. They create new worlds, new characters, and new narratives. While CAD models are used to imagine objects for use in our real world, CGI is used to imagine things impossible in our reality. Talking clownfish, armies of zombies, even the shivering breath of a doomed couple.

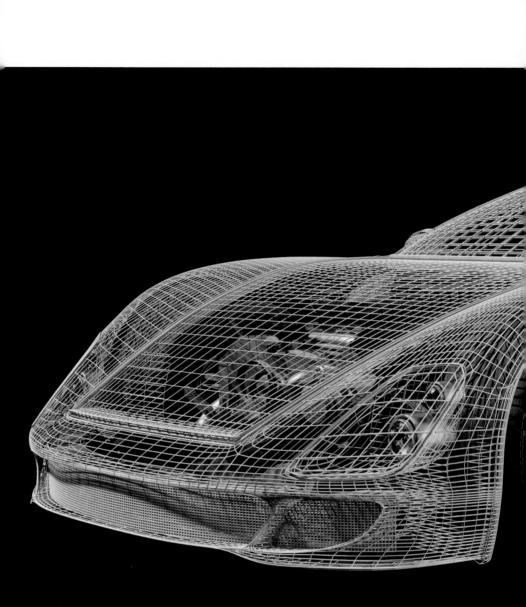

Today, car companies use CAD to
virtually test-drive their newest models.

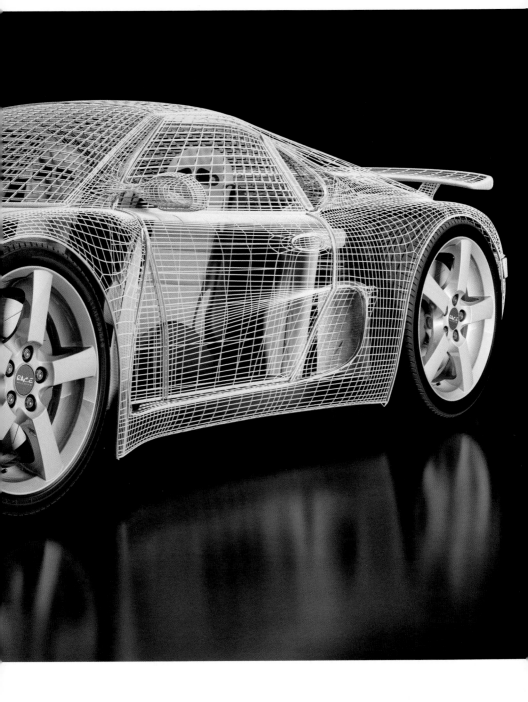

CAD and the FUTURE

Using CAD technologies to create an image means you can create a digital object that can be constantly changed and manipulated. This fact is perhaps the most clear in gaming, a prominent application for CGI and CAD. A video game like *Grand Theft Auto* is different every time you play it. Depending on what input you offer, the gameplay changes. The game is dependent on the viewer or user. While paintings continue to exist even if they are stored away in a closet where no one can see them, digital images are harder to imagine when they are not being used or viewed. They are dependent on input from us, which makes them a type of interactive art.

And it seems like new technology will take interaction to the next level. Virtual reality may be the next frontier for CAD, as filmmakers, designers, and artists quickly embrace developments in the technology. Either using a special 360-degree camera or CGI graphics, artists working in VR can create an **immersive** experience. As you turn your head, the images on the headset you wear turn with you, so you seem to be completely engulfed by the reality of the virtual world. Combining photography, filmmaking, and CGI, virtual reality began mostly as an application for immersive gaming experiences, but as technology has evolved, artists and filmmakers are beginning to explore how they can use this new medium for storytelling and art.

The *Guardian*, a UK newspaper, has created a virtual reality documentary called "6×9," titled for the size of a solitary confinement cell. When you put on the headset, you're transported to a tiny cell with a cot, toilet, four walls, and not much else. The experience of imprisonment in such a small space for twenty-three hours a day comes to life for the viewer because "being in" the cell is so much more powerful than seeing pictures of it. In this piece, virtual reality is used to reveal something about the harsh realities of the American prison system.

Even though, like Ivan Sutherland, it is impossible for us to see into the future and know how virtual reality will become integrated into both the art world and our daily lives, it seems certain that CAD and CGI will be an important part of designing the unimaginable worlds we will be able to explore without a passport or a rocket ship, just earphones and a video headset. Perhaps we will even approach the "ultimate display" outlined by Sutherland in the quote at the start of this chapter. Maybe CAD will be used to design a virtual world that is as real as this one, where "a bullet displayed in such a room would be fatal."

Perhaps this evolution is already underway, with CAD models at its center. If you make a detailed, completely accurate CAD model of a gun, until recently there had been no way to take that digital model and create the real thing. But with the invention of 3D printers, now you can take a digital 3D model— probably created using CAD software—and "print" it in plastic. In fact, in 2012 the first 3D printed gun, "The Liberator," was created and fired by the company Defense Distributed. While no one has been shot with a bullet fired from a 3D-printed gun yet, it seems that Sutherland's predictions may be coming true.

Digital technologies blur the lines between the virtual and the actual world, between representation and reality. CAD is mostly used for utilitarian purposes like drafting and modeling. CGI is mainly a tool of big-budget action and animated films. Yet it seems possible that as it becomes easier to use CAD and more and more people master it, the medium will evolve to become as essential to our daily life as drawing is. The first artists—cave painters and early sculptors—surely, like Sutherland, never imagined the wealth of images we would "live in" today. Those

"The Liberator," a gun made with a 3D printer

early works of art were often hidden away, but as technology advanced, images became more and more readily available. You probably have a poster or a painting hanging on the wall behind your head right now. Maybe in a thousand years, everyone will have the ability to be a CAD artist, taking impossible visions and projecting them into our shared reality.

A 3D printer in action

CHAPTER 6
Visions of the Future

n her book *A Field Guide to Getting Lost*, Rebecca Solnit says:

> Certainly for artists of all stripes, the unknown, the idea or the form or the tale that has not yet arrived, is what must be found. It is the job of artists to open doors and invite in prophesies, the unknown, the unfamiliar; it's where their work comes from, although its arrival signals the beginning of the long disciplined process of making it their own.

If we consider art in these terms—the known and the unknown—we may better understand what motivates humans to seek out, try to create, or look for beauty. We've seen that ancient civilizations used art as a means of connecting with the unknown, like the way ancient Egyptians represented the afterlife. In visual art, the *unknown* can also be considered the *unseen*.

It seems that the drive to make art is an essential part of human nature, not a human response to an external factors. What the earliest cave paintings, both in western Europe and the Maros-Pangkep Caves in Indonesia, reveal is that the common denominator in human creation of art is not competition, survival, or dominance, but humans themselves. Those early artists made art that still tells a story today. Issues of how to represent our three-dimensional world on a two-dimensional surface began then as well, and from the crossed legs of two bison at Lascaux evolved a complex history of perspective in art.

The problem of how to present space and motion is one that has challenged artists since the beginning of art. Now art itself can be in motion—in films, virtual reality headsets, and **kinetic sculpture**, our art has become almost alive with possibility. Just as a long-dead painter tried to represent buffalo streaming out, about to trample the viewer, artists today are looking for new and innovative ways to reproduce and represent reality.

Now innovations in the art world are increasingly focused on new technologies to represent three-dimensional forms. Virtual reality headsets and 3D printers allow artists to re-create the experience of viewing famous art, either through detailed scans and printed plastic, or through a complex camera and viewing system that takes the viewer to the art or subject virtually. These platforms are fast growing, but not all artists are embracing the new media.

3D PRINTING and ART

Maybe you've been to the Louvre and seen the *Winged Victory of Samothrace*, headless and armless, set on a pedestal at the top of a grand staircase, surrounded by tourists like admirers falling at her marble feet. Carved around 2,200 years ago, the woman's rich drapery seems to be blown back by a breeze, even though the sculpture is crafted from thousands of pounds of stone. If you've never had the privilege of seeing this sculpture in person, there is a new way of viewing art that is becoming increasingly popular: 3D printing. Using detailed scans of the sculpture, people who have access to a 3D printer can print a scale model, one twenty-fifth the size of the original, in plastic. MyMiniFactory, a company that offers 3D-printable files, recently launched Scan the World. Scan the World is a 3D scanning initiative, in the hopes that users would generate 3D files for every public sculpture and landmark in the world. It's an ambitious project with a goal of making famous artwork cheaply available to classrooms and communities. Scan the World also aims to make art available to the visually impaired, who can touch a 3D-printed sculpture. Now 3,650 sculptures have been archived and are freely accessible for printing.

A technology like 3D printing cannot match the experience of standing beneath the real *Winged Victory* sculpture. Printed plastic does not convey the grandeur, detail, and history of the sculpture, but it can be a useful tool in conserving art. In this case, because the technology is being used to create a copy, it is generally used to produce souvenirs, not high art. Yet there are contemporary artists who are creating exciting and groundbreaking work that would not have been possible without 3D printers.

TECHNOLOGY AND ACCESSIBILITY

As art moved from spiritual spaces like cathedrals into institutions like museums, the art world and its relationship to the common man also changed. Thanks to photography, images of famous artworks are more available than ever, but the proportion of the population that has actually seen these works in person is quite small. While almost everyone in a city would have attended church and seen the fabulous paintings—perhaps by Michelangelo or Leonardo—now the public's interaction with art has become more and

The *Winged Victory of Samothrace* and other iconic sculptures can be reproduced using 3D printers.

more virtual, through a computer screen. Museums and famous monuments are starting to document their spaces using virtual reality cameras, so you can travel to the Sistine Chapel without ever leaving your couch.

Issues of cost and availability dog some of these most recent innovations in art, like CAD, virtual reality, and 3D printers. While they are impressive and powerful tools to create new forms of art, the high cost of these platforms mean that they are unavailable to most users. A low-funded inner-city school might not be able to afford a decent computer lab to teach all of its students to use Word and Excel, let alone a 3D printer for students to practice with. To try to address this issue, some libraries have started to offer use of 3D printers, advanced cameras, and even virtual reality headsets like the Oculus Rift to their community. Thinking of new ways to make expensive technologies like this accessible to all opens exciting possibilities for the future of visual art.

HOLOGRAMS AND INSTAGRAM

Just as CAD and 3D printing are changing the definition of sculpture, digital technologies are revolutionizing photography. Though daguerreotypes are actually a scientifically complex way to translate light into an image on a page, holograms are an even more involved way to create an image. Holograms use lasers, lenses, and mirrors to create an exact 3D rendering of an object. While photographic cameras record a relatively small amount of data compared to the amount our eyes and brain process, holograms record something like a million trillion pixels. Our most advanced home TV displays have only about ten million pixels. (This is one reason that we are a long way off from true hologram experiences being broadcast into homes.)

In a true hologram, the image displayed on the screen is exactly the same as that in real life. All of the light that would be reflected back to our eyes, creating an image, say, of a Great Dane, is also captured in a hologram. So if you view the holographic screen from different angles, you would see the Great Dane from the side or front on, for example. It's a true 3D experience, and the only 3D display that doesn't require special glasses for viewing.

In fact, many of the images generally referred to as "holograms" are really tricks of lighting and screens. After a "hologram" of Tupac Shakur appeared onstage at Coachella in 2012, the media was abuzz with the potential to resurrect other dead celebrities using this technology. In fact, the Tupac seen onstage was a CGI creation, projected onto the stage using a Victorian-era visual trick called "Pepper's Ghost" after its inventor. A thin piece of transparent glass or film is positioned in front of the stage, so that a reflection of a person or screen below the stage appears to be standing on it. Not quite the same as a million-trillion-pixel holographic image.

Experts believe that as our technology advances, holograms may replace traditional photography. So instead of capturing a 2D representation of a scene with a camera, recording a fraction of the light the human eye sees, we will be able to create holograms that record all or almost all of the light our eyes would see, effectively preserving a "perfect" or complete image.

Another, more accessible innovation in the photography world is Instagram. This image-based social media platform has begun to transform galleries and how we consume art. Instagram photographers have begun to be recognized as artists in their own right. The International Center of

The "Pepper's Ghost" illusion involves a room the audience cannot see (*left*), a reflective surface (*green*), and a vantage point that manipulates viewers (*red*).

MOREHSHIN ALLAHYARI AND THE EVOLUTION OF ART

Morehshin Allahyari, an artist born in Iran who later immigrated to America, uses 3D printing and other digital tools in her work. For her project "Material Speculation: ISIS," she created 3D models of ancient artworks that ISIS has destroyed. They are semitranslucent, and embedded in each is a flash drive or memory card containing the 3D modeling files, images, and extensive research on each artifact. Of the project, Allahyari writes:

> "Material Speculation: ISIS" creates a practical and political possibility for artifact archival, while also proposing 3D printing technology as a tool both for resistance and documentation. It intends to use 3D printing as a process for repairing history and memory. [The project] goes beyond metaphoric gestures and digital and material forms of the artifacts by including a flash drive and a memory card inside the body of each 3D printed object. Like time capsules, each object is sealed and kept for future civilizations.

Allahyari's project is in some respects very similar to the Scan the World initiative, hoping to catalogue the great artworks of the world. But hers is seen as contemporary art, not as a hobby or way to re-create artworks for souvenirs. So what is the difference? What elevates Allahyari's work to the status of high art is the purpose and reasoning behind her work. She is not just creating 3D models that approximate ancient sculpture, but creating a new work, one that interacts with the way ISIS uses technology and social media to further its agenda. By fighting back against the erasure of pre-Islamic artwork using the digital domain, Allahyari is trying to beat ISIS at its own game, using 3D-printed art as her weapon.

Some artists, like visual artist Morehshin Allahyari, have incorporated 3D printers into their creative process.

Photography recently put on an exhibition called *Public, Private, Secret* that blended digital photography, paparazzi photos, Instagram, videos, and other contemporary genres together. Now instead of going to an intimidating gallery to consume photography or buy art, we can find it, and even buy it, right on our phones. Art, especially photography, is increasingly accessible for everyone.

But if anyone can take a high-quality photograph with his or her phone, then what distinguishes the artist from the hobbyist? This is a question that reappears again and again concerning contemporary art. As the tools of production and time to produce it are readily available to everyone, how do we define art, and who gets to make it? The answer some give, at its simplest, is that it is art if you say it is; the intention behind the piece is what makes it art. Others still claim that it is technical mastery and skill that makes an artist.

In the International Center of Photography show, the artist Doug Rickard exhibited a piece made from found footage of crimes and police violence uploaded from cell phones. According to writer Holland Cotter of the *New York Times*:

> Mr. Rickard collages excerpts from various postings into fictional narratives, notable less for their plotlines than for the atmosphere of danger they project. That atmosphere is similar to one generated by news media and the film industry, an adrenalin-fueled mood of fear, suspicion and emergency, encouraging violence.

The footage itself isn't art. It's something we all could create. But the way it is manipulated, collected, and displayed is art. As technology makes photography and art in general more accessible to all, it is the mind and the intention of the artist that matters. You can make art from anything. You just have to know how to make it say what you want it to.

VIRTUAL REALITY AND THE PROBLEM OF IMMERSION

As touched on in the chapter on CAD, virtual reality headsets and experiences are on the cresting wave of innovation. From journalism applications, like the *Guardian's* "6×9" project, to gaming to advertising, creators are using VR for more and more applications. Unfortunately, the technology is not very advanced. Facebook bought the Oculus VR headset company for $2 billion in 2014, but people at Oculus say their technology is at the same stage as the Apple II personal computer—which was a huge innovation for its time in 1977, but compared to today's computers is incredibly clunky and expensive. This means that VR devices have a long way to go before they are as used as much as the personal computer is today.

In an article called "Tripping Down the Virtual Reality Rabbit Hole," Farhad Manjoo at the *New York Times* brings up some important issues that trouble current VR experiences. He says that the headset covers your ears and eyes—when you put it on, you are, in a way, incapacitated and lose most of the sense that would be able to place you in your surroundings. You can't walk around when you wear a headset because you'll bump into things. You can't see your hands, and you lose the feel for where your body is positioned in space. It doesn't mesh well with how we like to interact with technology and our devices. We

ISIS destroyed the Temple of Bel in 2015. Innovative artists are using technology to ensure that landmarks like this Syrian temple live on.

watch a movie, check Facebook, and text on our phone, all at once. We don't prefer immersive experience, we prefer multitasking and moving quickly back and forth between activities. VR doesn't lend itself to multitasking. In fact, the purpose is to be totally swallowed up in the experience it transports you to. It can be disorienting and uncomfortable.

Now VR device manufacturers are starting to add special gloves the user can wear that enable the headset to project digital versions of your limbs in front of you, which is quite helpful for gaming applications. Even so, the VR world does not yet seem to have found the perfect application for their technology. Will it be used for a passive form of entertainment, like films, or an interactive one, like gaming? Or will it replace photojournalism as the ultimate way to bring the experience of really being there to newsreaders? Will it be used by CGI artists to create immersive experiences in new and amazing worlds, or will it be used by storytellers and journalists to reflect reality back to us? Even the name of the system, "virtual reality," suggests the sometimes conflicting possibilities for the medium. On the one hand we have "virtual," as in unreal. On the other, "reality." Will this technology change how we understand reality? Maybe putting on a headset and circling the sculpture *Winged Victory of Samothrace* virtually will be seen to be as "true" as really being there. But what about how the VR programs are often manipulated? Even the "6×9" project that transports the viewer to a solitary confinement cell was not filmed in a real cell but was created using CGI. Is it still a "real" experience? Despite virtual reality's flaws and the questions surrounding its applications, there is no doubt that virtual reality is here to stay.

Virtual reality, holograms, and 3D printing also have uses outside of the art world. All of these technologies are used by the advertising industry. They are used to display commercial art, like a holographic ad for sneakers or a VR experience advertising a posh hotel or expensive sports car. Today, the divide between what would be considered fine art and commercial art has become blurred. This blurring is nothing new, though. In the 1960s, pop artist Andy Warhol took everyday images—like a Campbell's soup can—and made them into fine art. But as our world has become more and more cluttered with images, from TV to cereal box graphics to ads on Facebook, our eyes are assaulted by commercial art meant not to open our eyes or transport us, but to get us to buy a product or service. There are some artists, however, who have been pushing the boundaries, using virtual reality, holograms, and 3D printing not with the goal of selling the public something but instead to expand our minds, question the establishment, and create pieces of stunning beauty.

Inventions in art bring us closer to each other. Cave paintings communicated ancient messages and were a part of important cultural memory. The sketchbook allowed artists to work out ideas. Photography enabled us to paint pictures with light, capturing memories and creating art out of the scenes around us. Artist Morehshin Allahyari fights ISIS's destruction using 3D printing. Perhaps thousands of years from now, an archaeologist will find one of her sculptures, a living memory of a piece of art destroyed and brought back to life by an invention in art.

GLOSSARY

aperture The opening, in a camera and other optical instruments, through which light enters.

Archaic period In ancient Greece, the time when artists adopted a more natural style and made advances in technique.

beau ideal Ideal beauty, or a model of perfection.

bitumen of Judea Asphalt used in early photography for its light-sensitive properties.

bodhisattvas A figure in a branch of Buddhishm called Mahayana, a boddhisattva is someone who could achieve enlightenment but chooses to wait in order to help others become enlightened.

camera obscura A dark chamber with a lens aperture that was the first device that could project the image of a real external scene onto another surface.

chiaroscuro Shading technique used to portray light and shadows.

daguerreotype An image captured on a metal plate; the product of the first photographic process.

deities Gods or goddesses.

depiction An image or likeness.

ephemeral Anything that will not last. In art, performances that are not recorded are ephemeral as are any sculptures or paintings made from materials that break down, decay, or are intentionally destroyed.

exposure The amount of light that reaches photographic film (or another light-sensative material) when taking a picture.

foreground The part of a scene or picture that is closest to the viewer.

foreshortening A perspective technique used in visual art to convey three-dimensional space.

gestural Paint brush strokes that are applied using exaggerated physical gestures.

Hellenistic Art produced in ancient Greece between 323 BCE to 31 BCE. Hellenistic sculpture generally shows historical or mythical figures.

heroic realism From the classical Greek period, a realistic portrayal heightened by extraordinary beauty or a dramatic moment.

immersive Art that creates an entire environment for the viewer.

kinetic sculpture Sculpture that featurres moving parts. Some kinetic sculptures are meant to be interactive.

Kodak camera A user-friendly camera with roll film technology, cited as the device that made amateur photography possible.

kouroi/korai Greek statues of young men and women, respectively, from the archaic period.

latent image An invisible image on exposed film.

linear perspective The principle in visual art that objects recede and grow smaller in the distance, with exact mathematical rules governing the optical phenomenon.

mikkyo The Japanese term for Esoteric Buddhism.

Mohists A group of ancient Chinese philosophers who designed the camera prototype during the fifth century BCE.

nirvana The enlightened state of being in Buddhism that, when achieved, frees a person from the endless cycle of death and rebirth.

ochre Yellow to reddish-brown paint made of fine powder and water.

pinhole camera A primitive camera made with a dark box that uses a small hole as an aperture instead of a lens.

sfumato A shading technique developed by Leonardo da Vinci to soften the outline of objects in drawing and painting.

shamanistic A method of communicating with the spiritual world through rituals.

Venus figurines Small statues of the female form, symbolizing fertility or a female goddess.

FURTHER INFORMATION

BOOKS

Buchholz, Elke Linda, Gerhard Bühler, Karoline Hille, Susanne Kaeppele, and Irina Stotland. *Art: A World History*. New York: Abrams, 2007.

Christianson, Scott. *100 Diagrams That Changed the World: From the Earliest Cave Paintings to the Innovation of the iPod*. New York: Plume, 2012.

Cumming, Robert. *Art: A Visual History*. London: DK, 2015.

Volvovski, Jenny, Julia Rothman, and Matt Lamothe. *The Where, the Why, and the How: 75 Artists Illustrate Wondrous Mysteries of Science*. San Francisco: Chronicle Books, 2012.

VIDEOS

Ivan Sutherland Sketchpad Demonstration
https://youtu.be/6orsmFndx_o
This 1964 footage shows Ivan Sutherland demonstrating his Sketchpad program for a reporter. The light pen and graphical interface were completely revolutionary at the time.

6×9: A Virtual Experience of Solitary Confinement
https://youtu.be/odcsxUbVyZA
If you have Google Cardboard or a VR headset, use that to view this video. If not, you can scroll around 360 degrees at the link above and experience a cell that inmates in solitary confinement are kept in for twenty-three hours a day.

WEBSITES

The Bradshaw Foundation
http://www.bradshawfoundation.com/france/
The Bradshaw Foundation is dedicated to preserving the cave paintings in France. Find out more about the early art found at Lascaux, Chauvet, and other sites.

The Met Artist Project
http://artistproject.metmuseum.org/6
Contemporary artists tour the Metropolitan Museum of Art, discussing their favorite works. In the short videos that make this web series, you can see works of art from an artist's perspective.

Museum of Modern Art: Red Studio
http://www.moma.org/interactives/redstudio
Learn more about modern art and what it's like to be an artist today with the interactive project developed by the Museum of Modern Art for young adults. This website offers interviews, activities, contests, and behind-the-scenes access to an art museum.

Visual Art Throughout History
http://arthistory.about.com/od/famous_names/u/artists.htm
Read biographies of artists, view famous works of art, and explore a timeline of art history on this About.com page.

BIBLIOGRAPHY

"About Creating 3D Wireframe Models." Autodesk Knowledge Network. December 16, 2015. https://knowledge.autodesk.com/support/autocad/ getting-started/caas/CloudHelp/cloudhelp/2016/ENU/ AutoCAD-Core/files/GUID-84E193D7-A18D-4EE2-B978-19E4AFBCAEEC-htm.html.

Allahyari, Morehshin. "Material Speculation: ISIS." Retrieved June 23, 2016. http://www.morehshin.com/ material-speculation-isis.

Aubert, M., A. Brumm, M. Ramli, T. Sutikna, E. W. Saptomo, B. Hakim, M. J. Morwood, G. D.

Van Den Bergh, L. Kinsley, and A. Dosseto. "Pleistocene Cave Art from Sulawesi, Indonesia." *Nature* 514, no. 7521 (2014): 223–27. doi:10.1038/nature13422.

Aujoulat, Norbert. *Lascaux: Movement, Space, and Time.* New York: H. N. Abrams, 2005.

Bambach, Carmen. "Leonardo da Vinci (1452–1519)." Heilbrunn Timeline of Art History. October 2002. http://www.metmuseum.org/toah/hd/leon/hd_leon.htm.

———. "Renaissance Drawings: Material and Function." Heilbrunn Timeline of Art History. October 2002. http://www.metmuseum.org/toah/hd/leon/hd_leon. htm.

Benigni, Helen. "The Emergence of the Goddess." In *The Mythology of Venus: Ancient Calendars and Archaeoastronomy*. Edited by Helen Benigni. Lanham, MD: UPA, 2013.

Burton, Robert. "Ivan Sutherland." A. M. Turing Award. Retrieved June 03, 2016. http://amturing.acm.org/award_winners/sutherland_3467412.cfm.

Cotter, Holland. "Photography's Shifting Identity in an Insta-World." *New York Times*, June 23, 2016. http://www.nytimes.com/2016/06/24/arts/design/review-photographys-shifting-identity-in-an-insta-world.html.

Gogh, Vincent van. *Delphi Masters of Art: Complete Works of Vincent Van Gogh* Delphi Publishing Limited, 2011. Kindle e-book.

Goldsworthy, Andy. "Sculptor Turns Rain, Ice And Trees Into 'Ephemeral Works.'" Interview by Terry Gross. *Fresh Air*. NPR. October 8, 2015.

Heiferman, Marvin. *Photography Changes Everything*. New York: Aperture, 2012.

Hemingway, Colette, and Seán Hemingway. "The Art of Classical Greece (ca. 480–323 B.C.)." Heilbrunn Timeline of Art History. January 2008. http://www.metmuseum.org/toah/hd/tacg/hd_tacg.htm

Hughes, Virginia. "Were the First Artists Mostly Women?" *National Geographic*. October 10, 2013. http://news.nationalgeographic.com/news/2013/10/131008-women-handprints-oldest-neolithic-cave-art/

Jones, Jonathan. "Leonardo da Vinci's Notebooks Are Beautiful Works of Art in Themselves." *Guardian*, February 12, 2013. https://www.theguardian.com/artanddesign/jonathanjonesblog/2013/feb/12/leonardo-da-vici-notebooks-art.

King, Ross. *Art: Over 2,500 Works from Cave to Contemporary*. New York: DK., 2008.

Manjoo, Farhad. "Tripping Down a Virtual Reality Rabbit Hole." *New York Times*, June 22, 2016. http://www.nytimes.com/2016/06/23/technology/tripping-down-a-virtual-rabbit-hole.html.

McCracken, Harry. "A Talk with Computer Graphics Pioneer Ivan Sutherland." Time, April 12, 2013. http://techland.time.com/2013/04/12/a-talk-with-computer-graphics-pioneer-ivan-sutherland.

Mcdermott, Leroy. "Self-Representation in Upper Paleolithic Female Figurines." *Current Anthropology* 37, no. 2 (1996): 227–75. doi:10.1086/204491.

Payne, Alina, ed. *Vision and Its Instruments: Art, Science, and Technology in Early Modern Europe*. University Park, PA: Penn State University Press. 2015.

Solnit, Rebecca. *A Field Guide to Getting Lost*. New York: Penguin, 2006.

Sutherland, Ivan. "Augmented Reality: The Ultimate Display." *Wired*, 1965.

Loevgren, Sven. *The Genesis of Modernism: Seurat, Gauguin, Van Gogh, and French Symbolism in the 1880s.* Bloomington: Indiana University Press, 1971.

Thompson, Helen. "Rock (Art) of Ages: Indonesian Cave Paintings Are 40,000 Years Old." *Smithsonian*, October 8, 2014. http://www.smithsonianmag.com/science-nature/rockart-ages-indonesian-cave-paintings-are-40000-years-old-180952970/?no-ist.

Wilford, John Noble. "Full-Figured Statuette, 35,000 Years Old, Provides New Clues to How Art Evolved." *New York Times*, May 13, 2009. http://www.nytimes.com/2009/05/14/science/14venus.html.

INDEX

ABOUT the AUTHOR

CORY MACPHERSON is a writer and poet currently living in North Carolina. After attending Elon University and University of North Carolina at Wilmington, she received a degree in creative writing. MacPherson continued her study of creative writing, receiving an MFA in poetry writing at the University of North Carolina at Greensboro.